Y0-ELL-067

BLACK HEROES
Coloring book

BLM 💚 Illustrated by Ingrid Zúñiga

NONVIOLENT KING
with a dream

⤜ Martin Luther King Jr. ⤛

THE MOTHER OF THE

Freedom movement

❧ Rosa Parks ❧

IF YOU'RE NOT READY
TO DIE FOR IT,
put the word 'freedom'
out of your vocabulary

Malcolm X

One of the most
IMPORTANT AMERICAN
leaders of the
20th CENTURY

Ella Baker

BECAUSE SHE KNEW WHY
the caged bird sings

Maya Angelou

The Voice of
HARLEM RENAISSANCE

Zora Neale Hurston

Defeated apartheid
AFTER 27 YEARS IN PRISON

❧ Nelson Mandela ❧

First African woman
TO WIN A NOBEL PRIZE

Wangari Maathai

First African-American
PRESIDENT
OF THE UNITED STATES

❧ Barack Obama ❧

Abolitionist
who would unite
with anybody to do right
AND WITH NOBODY
TO DO WRONG

Frederick Douglass

MOTHER OF
African-American
Poetry

❧ Phyllis Wheatley ❧

Reggaeman, Rastafarian
AND ROCK AND ROLL
HALL OF FAMER

Bob Marley

YOUNG, GIFTED AND BLACK
little girl blue

Nina Simone

Queen of Soul

❦ Aretha Franklin ❧

The prince
OF SOUL

⤞ Marvin Gaye ⤝

The Father of
ROCK AND ROLL

Chuck Berry

The Architect
OF ROCK AND ROLL

⚘ Little Richard ⚘

The greatest
instrumentalist
IN THE HISTORY OF ROCK MUSIC

Jimmy Hendrix

King
OF THE BLUES

BB King

THE GREATEST

Muhammad Ali

HAMMERIN

⤙ Hank Aaron ⤚

THE G.O.A.T.

Michael Jordan

The Queen

Oprah Winfrey

Made in United States
Troutdale, OR
10/03/2025

35081745R00015